The Tapestry Of Time

Threads of Joy and Sorrow

Manu

India | USA | UK

Dedication

To my loving husband Neeraj,

You are the quiet strength behind my every storm, the calm in my chaos, and the light that led me through my darkest nights. When life tested me with loss, you held my hand and taught me the art of letting go—not with despair, but with grace. You showed me that acceptance is not surrender, that healing is not forgetting, and that even in sorrow, love never truly leaves us.

You taught me how to face my fears, to believe in myself when I felt broken, and to see the beauty in a world that once seemed cruel. Because of you, I have learned to embrace joy, to seek out the good, and to tap into happiness, even in the smallest moments. This book is a reflection of that journey—a journey I would have never navigated without your love, your patience, and your unwavering faith in me.

With all my heart,
Manu

Preface

*Life is a mosaic of moments—some bright with joy,
others shadowed by pain. In these pages, I have poured
my heart, tracing the bittersweet journey of loss, love,
healing, and hope.*

*For years, I struggled with goodbyes I never wanted to
say, with dreams that slipped through my fingers before
they could bloom. But in those moments of heartbreak, I
found an anchor—my husband. He taught me that grief
does not define us, that loss is not the end but a
transformation, and that happiness is always within
reach if we choose to see it.*

*This book is not just my story; it is a testament to
resilience, to love that heals, and to the belief that even
after the deepest sorrow, life still holds immeasurable
beauty. To my husband, who taught me the art of
acceptance and the power of hope—this book is, in many
ways, because of you.*

*May these words bring comfort to anyone who has
walked a similar path and remind them that, no matter
how dark the night, the dawn always follows.*

With gratitude,
Manu

Acknowledgements

To my husband—my safe place, my greatest teacher, and the love of my life. Thank you for standing beside me when I was at my weakest, for holding me when words failed, and for reminding me that life, despite its losses, is still breathtakingly beautiful. You have been my greatest lesson in love, in resilience, and in seeing light even when the world felt dark.

And to my son*—the one who changed the very definition of life for me. You erased every sorrow, filled every empty space in my heart, and became my brightest ray of hope. You are my miracle, my joy, and the reason I believe in the magic of life again. Watching you grow is my greatest privilege, and loving you is my life's purest blessing.*

To my sisters—the strongest women I know. Together, we have faced life's storms, walked through fire, and carried the weight of heartbreaks that could have broken us. Yet, here we stand, having fought through our share of disappointments, sorrows, grief, losses, and traumas— only to find joy waiting for us on the other side. I am grateful for every moment we have lifted each other up, for every tear we have wiped away, and for every laugh we have shared despite it all. You are my sisters by birth, but my soulmates in strength.

To my little angels who never made it earthside—your presence was brief, but your love is eternal. You taught me the depths of a mother's heart, and though you are not here, you live in every beat of mine.

To my family and friends, who lifted me with their love and patience—you have been my pillars, my sounding boards, and my sources of endless strength.

To every reader who finds a piece of themselves in these words—may you find comfort, courage, and the strength to believe that joy is still yours to claim.

And to life itself—thank you for the lessons, the heartbreaks, and the endless miracles that make this journey worth taking.

With all my love,
Manu

1. The Man Who Chose Me

He saw a light when I saw none,
Called me special, his only one.
While I feared the world, too scared to try,
He gave me wings and taught me to fly.

I walked on roads, unsure, afraid,
He held my hand, yet let me wade.
"Take the risk," he'd always say,
But played it safe in his own way.

To him, I'm perfect—flaws and all,
An average girl, yet standing tall.
The world's best, in his kind eyes,
A treasure rare, a precious prize.

He was the man all longed to find,
A heart so pure, a soul so kind.
If more like him, the world could be,
No woman would cry in misery.

With every breath, I pray, I trust,
That fate stays kind, that love stays just.
For luck was mine the day he knew,
Of all the hearts, he chose me too.

2. The Silent Battle

Born a daughter, not a son,
A quiet sigh, the celebrations—none.
Three of us, yet still alone,
In our own house, never a throne.

A mother who loved, yet never knew,
The silent battles that only grew.
A father fading, lost in time,
While we stood strong, yet climbed, yet climbed.

"Be like her," they'd always say,
"Talk like this, don't walk that way."
Not pretty enough, nor wise nor bright,
Just an echo, hidden from sight.

No one asked, "What do you feel?"
Mental health—was that even real?
Tears were weak, silence was grace,
Pain was hidden, no room for space.

An uncle's stare, a shadowed fear,
Yet no one saw, no one came near.
Fighting alone, with no one to trust,
Buried deep, yet rise I must.

Failed and broken, but not yet gone,
In books I found where I belonged.
A spark, a dream, a path so wide,
No more hiding, no more denied.

Today I stand, no more unseen,
Not just a daughter—but a queen.
Mental health is real, I say,
For every girl to find her way.

And if tomorrow brings more light,
Let daughters grow, let them take flight.
No sighs, no shame, just endless pride,
An equal world, where none must hide.

3. A letter to my Son-shine

They speak of daughters, lifting them high,
Teaching them wings to touch the sky.
But as I hold my little boy near,
I wonder—do they see him clear?

A child so pure, a heart so kind,
Yet the world tells him, "Stay behind."
"You're privileged, strong—don't you cry,"
But why can't he ask the reasons why?

I teach him love, I teach him grace,
To walk with kindness, not in a race.
Yet in this world where voices rise,
Must his be lost, must he disguise?

Feminism fights for what is right,
For every girl to stand in light.
But let us not, in fixing wrong,
Create a space where boys don't belong.

For justice means a world that's fair,
Where all can dream, where all can share.
Not lifting one while pulling another,
But walking together—as sister and brother.

So I pray, as he grows tall,
Let him be gentle, let him stand tall.
Not afraid to feel, to speak, to be,
A boy who's kind, yet strong and free.

Let's build a world where all can shine,
Where sons and daughters both define—
A future bright, a world so new,
*Where love and respect belong to **all** too.*

4. The Healing Touch of Love

I was broken, lost in the night,
A fading star, no spark, no light.
A heart weighed down by scars unseen,
A soul unsure of what love could mean.

Then came you—so calm, so true,
With hands that held, with eyes that knew.
No need for words, no grand display,
Just quiet love that chose to stay.

You saw the cracks, yet loved me whole,
Your warmth, your trust—my weary soul.
No questions asked, no price to pay,
Just love that healed in its own way.

Through every storm, through every fall,
You stood beside, you took it all.
Not to fix, not to mend,
But just to love, just to send—

A silent promise, strong and deep,
That love like this is ours to keep.
For where love stays, pain must leave,
And hearts once broken learn to breathe.

5. The Two Lives of Me

By morning light, I wear my crown,
A leader, a worker, I won't back down.
Deadlines call, the clock won't wait,
A world of tasks, a world so great.

Yet in my heart, another beat,
Tiny hands, pattering feet.
A whispered "Mama," soft and sweet,
The love that makes my life complete.

One world demands, one softly pleads,
Both my own, both my needs.
Juggling dreams, chasing time,
Guilt and pride in tangled rhyme.

Late-night meetings, stories untold,
Hugs I miss, hands I hold.
Strength in chaos, love so vast,
A race with time that runs too fast.

But in their eyes, I find my way,
A reason to fight, to rise each day.
For in these roles—so fierce, so free,
*Lives a mother, lives **all of me**.*

6. The Fear I Cannot Speak

I see the silver in your hair,
The slowing steps, the distant stare.
The hands that once held mine so tight,
Now tremble soft in evening light.

I hear the wisdom in your tone,
Stories etched in time alone.
Yet in my heart, a whisper stays,
A silent fear that never fades.

What if one day, I call your name,
And only echoes speak the same?
What if the laughter, warm and bright,
Fades too soon into the night?

I hold your hand, but time moves fast,
Nothing mortal is meant to last.
Yet I pray for moments, days, and years,
More time to fight these silent fears.

So, I won't wait for days unknown,
I'll cherish you, I'll make it shown.
For love remains, though time may bend,
And never truly meets an end.

7. The Little Joys of Life

A cup of chai at dawn so bright,
With newspaper rustling in golden light.
Neighbors chatting by the gate,
As mornings rush, yet never late.

The whistle of the pressure pot,
Spices dancing in the hot.
A tiffin packed with love and care,
A mother's way to say, "Take care!"

The honking streets, the crowded train,
Yet laughter shared in monsoon rain.
Bargaining hard at the vendor's stall,
Over coriander, fresh and tall.

An evening walk with talks so deep,
Children's giggles, memories to keep.
TV blaring, dad's old tales,
As mom folds clothes and checks the mails.

Sunday calls to cousins far,
Plans of weddings, dreams bizarre.
Homemade sweets, a festive beat,
The joy of eating with hands, not neat!

No fancy trips, no grand delight,
Yet hearts are warm, and smiles are bright.
For in small joys, life does gleam,
A simple life, a priceless dream.

8. What We Found, What We Lost

Once, we lived in a room so small,
Yet love and laughter filled it all.
No fancy walls, no space to hide,
But hearts were warm, and dreams grew wide.

Evenings spent on rooftops high,
Counting stars in the open sky.
No rush, no race, just simple cheer,
A life so full, yet so near.

Then we chased, and then we ran,
For bigger homes, a grander plan.
From narrow lanes to avenues wide,
From whispered talks to calls confined.

Now weekends come, now weekends go,
Discussions wait, as deadlines grow.
Rooms are plenty, time is not,
In this grand house, what have we got?

The old tea stall, the friendly chat,
The joy of less—where is that?
Can we rewind, can we go back,
Or is it too late to change the track?

Maybe life is meant to change,
To stretch, to shift, to rearrange.
Yet deep inside, a voice still calls,
Can we live with less—and still have it all?

And so the mind debates and fights,
Through restless days and sleepless nights.
Yet life moves on, we chase, we strive,
Seeking more, while just trying to live.

9. Am I Outdated?

Am I outdated, lost in time,
In a world where screens now shine?
Where texts replace a heartfelt call,
And paperbacks fade from the mall?

I drape my saree, pleats so neat,
While sneakers race on hurried feet.
My home is filled with colors bright,
Handmade crafts, warm lamp light.

A rangoli glows at my doorstep wide,
As digital art takes the pride.
Mornings hum with chants so deep,
Not playlists new, but prayers I keep.

I don't know Coldplay, the latest trend,
Nor hashtags that the young defend.
Their lingo flies right past my ear,
Yet my world remains bright and clear.

Maybe I'm old-school, set in my way,
But warmth in touch will never decay.
For in a world that rushes fast,
Some old ways are meant to last.

10. You, My Calm in the Storm

When the world rushes, lost in race,
You walk steady, keeping pace.
No storm, no noise can shake your ground,
In your presence, peace is found.

While I chase, while I run,
You remind me—life's not done.
No need to hurry, no need to fear,
With you beside, the path is clear.

You hold the answers, soft yet strong,
A quiet wisdom, a heart full of song.
Where I see chaos, you find a way,
Turning worries into light each day.

You are the stillness, the steady tide,
The voice of reason by my side.
In your warmth, the world feels bright,
A place of love, of endless light.

Perhaps the world is kind and true,
Because of souls like yours, so few.
You are my anchor, my heart's own guide,
My calm, my love, my endless pride.

11. A Love That Grew With Us

We were just kids, wild and free,
Two hearts tangled in destiny.
At twenty-one, love took its flight,
Hiding, sneaking, stolen nights.

No fancy dates, no grand display,
Just street-side chai and dreams to sway.
Sunday movies, the same old song,
Yet with you, it felt so strong.

You pushed me hard, made me strive,
Held my hand, helped me thrive.
But oh, the fights—one-sided, of course,
My jealousy, your calm discourse.

I'd pout when you taught my friends,
While you laughed, knowing it'd mend.
Five years apart, yet love stood tall,
Miles never mattered at all.

From silly jokes to quiet tears,
We've built this love through all these years.
No matter how much I drive you insane,
With you, love's only grown—never wane.

Through time, through trials, here we stand,
Side by side, hand in hand.
A love that bloomed, still shining bright,
My heart, my home, my forever light.

12. Three Sisters

Three little girls, hands held tight,
Walking alone through endless night.
No guiding voice, no path to see,
Just shadows tall, no place to flee.

Lost in a world that judged their face,
Too dark, too plain, too little grace.
Confidence stolen, words held back,
Yet together, they filled what life did lack.

Secrets whispered, fears untold,
Monsters lurked in stories old.
Through silent screams and hidden scars,
They found their strength in broken parts.

No hand, no shield, no mentor, no guide,
They fought their battles side by side.
Shamed for simply being born,
Yet from the dust, they rose reborn.

Yet through the years, they sought in vain,
Validation to ease their pain.
Waiting for praise, proving their worth,
Forgetting their joy, their place on this earth.

Wasted years in others' eyes,
Chasing approval, drowning in lies.
But all along, they stood so tall,
Not seeing their greatness, not seeing it all.

And now in their forties, they finally see,
The past is gone, but they are free.
Healing wounds, rebuilding ties,
Sisters forever, through lows and highs.

For through the storms, through fire and cold,
They stood as one—three hearts, one soul.

13. Let's Celebrate Each Other

Not rivals, not foes, but sisters in grace,
Lifting each other, finding our place.

No race to win, no war to fight,
Together we shine, stronger than light.

Her success is not my defeat,
Her journey different, yet just as sweet.

Let's cheer for dreams, big and wide,
Stand as a force, side by side.

No judgments, no whispers, no silent stares,
Just hands to hold in love and care.

For every girl who's felt alone,
Let's be the strength, the kindness shown.

Rise, my sister, break every chain,

Let's dance in joy, not drown in pain.

Celebrate each win, each fall, each flight,
For when we stand together—
We are pure light. ✧

14. The Love-Hate Relation

We grew up together, side by side,
A rollercoaster of love and pride.
From stolen chocolates to bedtime tales,
From playful pranks to heartfelt wails.

One moment, we'd laugh until we cried,
The next, a battle—no one's side.
"You took my book!" "You lost my shoe!"
Oh, the fights we constantly knew!

Yet through the noise and silly feuds,
A love unspoken always brewed.
You stood beside me, strong and tall,
My first best friend, despite it all.

When life got rough and nights felt long,
You were the strength that kept me strong.
Through highs and lows, through dark and bright,
You were my anchor, my guiding light.

Years may pass, we may drift away,
Chasing dreams in lands far away.
But deep inside, we always know,
This bond of ours will only grow.

For no one else could take your place,
No love like ours, no warm embrace.
From childhood fights to memories true,
Dear sibling, my heart beats for you. ❤

15. Lost in the Chase

The narrow lanes of my old hometown,
Where laughter echoed, never worn down.
The smell of rain on dusty streets,
Barefoot runs, no rush, no beats.

Evenings spent at the local bazaar,
Haggling over bangles, dreaming afar.
The school bell's ring, the playground calls,
Writing names on dusty walls.

Teenage dreams in a simple space,
Rolling skirts up, matching grace.
Stealing perfumes from mom's drawer,
Wet hair flipping at the door.

Sneaking glances, hoping to see,
The colony boys noticing me.
Kohl-lined eyes, a lipstick trace,
Feeling grown-up, lost in the race.

Uncontrolled giggles, scoldings loud,
Yet, life felt simple, free, and proud.
No filters, no rehearsed delight,
Just hearts unburdened, spirits light.

But dreams were woven in city lights,
Pulled away by distant sights.
Suitcases packed, we left behind,
The roots once tied to heart and mind.

Now smiles are measured, laughter tamed,
Success and stress, so well-named.
Weekends planned, moments rare,
No stolen perfumes, no carefree air.

The urge to go back tugs me still,
Yet dreams push forward, against my will.
Between what was and what must be,
I'm stuck between the past and me.

Would I trade the life I chase,
For the childhood I can't replace?
Maybe one day, I'll find my way,
Back to the town where my heart stays.

16. Breaking the Chains

A report card once sealed my fate,
A single failure, a house of hate.
A trembling child, a silent plea,
Why was my worth a grade to see?

The slap, the shame, the endless cries,
The fear of failing, the silent ties.
They said it's love, they said it's right,
Discipline wrapped in painful might.

But did that beating shape my way?
Did it push me to where I stay?
I stand here strong, I made my name,
Yet the scars within still burn the same.

We were the children who bore the weight,
Of anger masked as parents' fate.
Unstructured rules, the iron hand,
Bound by customs we didn't understand.

But we are the bridge, the turning tide,
Breaking patterns, standing wide.
No more fear in a child's bright eyes,
No more shame in failure's guise.

It's okay to stumble, to miss the mark,
To find their light within the dark.
No grace marks define their worth,
No perfect scores decide their mirth.

Discipline is love, not a raised hand,
Confidence isn't built by cruel demands.
Racism in jest, the taunting shame,
Won't toughen souls, won't win the game.

We parent with peace, not with fear,
We listen now, we hold them near.
Mental health is not a tale,
It's the strength that makes one sail.

Born in the '80s, we break the chains,
Undo the trauma, erase the stains.
We raise our voices, we choose to stand,
For a world where love holds every hand.

17. The Power of Letting Go

I held on tight, knuckles white,
Chasing shadows, gripping light.
The past like chains wrapped around,
Every echo, every sound.

I traced old wounds, read old scars,
The girl who hid behind closed doors, afar.
The one who feared not being enough,
Fighting battles, silent but tough.

The child who failed, the girl unseen,
The woman who struggled to fit in between.
The one who worked, who loved, who lost,
Who paid the price, who bore the cost.

From one-room walls to city lights,
From whispered doubts to fearless flights.
From love in secret, stolen days,
To growing strong in life's own ways.

The tears of longing for a home left behind,
Old friends, lost time, memories intertwined.
The stolen perfumes, the rolling skirts,
Teenage dreams and innocent flirts.

The mother now who holds her child,
Soft, unwavering, fierce yet mild.
Breaking patterns, healing pain,
No slaps, no shame, no guilt's refrain.

I carried burdens, I wore the weight,
But I chose to rewrite my fate.
Not erased, not thrown away,
Just set down to find my way.

The sun felt warmer, the air more free,
The world no longer pulling me.
For when I chose to finally grow,
I found my wings in letting go.

18. Starting Over

They said, "She won't make it, she's bound to fall,"
A girl with dreams, too fragile, too small.
Each stumble became a whispered shame,
Every failure, a scar with my name.

They taught me silence, they clipped my wings,
Told me to settle for smaller things.
But fire within refused to die,
Even when tears blurred my sky.

I fell a hundred, a thousand times,
Lost my battles, lost my rhymes.
Called too weak, too bold, too much,
Yet none could break my spirit's touch.

With trembling hands, I wrote anew,
A story fierce, a path so true.
Not bound by norms, not chained by past,
I found my strength, I rose at last.

For every girl who's told she's less,
Know you hold the power to impress.
Fall, but rise, again, again—
No loss is final, no fight in vain.

Starting over is not defeat,
It's courage strong, it's heart that beats.
So wear your scars, let the world see,
A girl reborn—wild, fierce, and free.

19. My Greatest Blessing

In a world that rushes, you stand so still,
With a heart so vast, with love to fill.
A husband, a father, a son so true,
A friend so rare—men like you are few.

Through days of struggle, through times so lean,
You smiled and said, "We'll chase our dream."
And when fortune knocked upon our door,
You stayed the same, wanting no more.

Never once did you question or complain,
Through sunshine bright or pouring rain.
If things went right, you credited me,
If things went wrong, you took the plea.

With little ones, you laugh and play,
Their hero, their sunshine on a cloudy day.
With elders, you listen, respect so deep,
Their comfort, their warmth, their hands you keep.

So shy, yet charming in every way,
With quiet grace, you steal the day.
Dancing to my tunes, though steps unknown,
Yet making my heart your very own.

And when you tease, with that loving smirk,
"Hai mere kandhe se chhoti,
Par baithi rehti hai mere sar pe,"
I know I am home, where love will stay.

A blessing, a gift, my heart's delight,
With you, my world is forever bright.
No poem, no words could quite explain,
How lucky I am to share your name.

20. You Will Always Have a Choice

At every turn, in every fight,
A choice awaits in dark or light.
To rise again or stay behind,
To free your soul or chain your mind.

Give up the dream or try once more,
Stay by the shore or sail for more.
Dwell in the past or heal the pain,
Lose yourself or rise again.

Seek the world's nod or stand up tall,
Crave their praise or need none at all.
Measure worth by fleeting fame,
Or know yourself beyond a name.

Let failure break or wisdom grow,
Hold on to hurt or let it go.
Drown in doubt or dare to see,
You own your fate—you hold the key.

No path is set, no step is blind,
The power is yours, within your mind.
So choose with heart, choose with grace,
For every choice will shape your place.

21. The Happy Me

I wake to mornings soft and bright,
With golden hues and peaceful light.
No rush, no race, no endless chase,
Just simple joys in life's embrace.

Happiness is a Sunday slow,
With scattered toys in a carefree flow.
A kitchen warm with love and spice,
A meal cooked once, but shared twice.

A movie night, a playful fight,
For the remote, who wins tonight?
An intense game of Ludo bold,
Racing home, the thrill unfolds.

An evening walk, the sunset glows,
A world at peace, my heart just knows.
No regrets, no weight, no strain,
Just love that falls like gentle rain.

I've left behind the restless run,
Priorities set, the chase undone.
Life is simple, life is kind,
Contentment glows within my mind.

I'm grateful now for all I see,
For love, for laughter, for being me.
A life so slow, yet full and bright,
Where happiness blooms in quiet light.

www.ingramcontent.com/pod-product-compliance
Lightning Source LLC
LaVergne TN
LVHW021259200726